If I speak in the tong

love, I am only a res..

If I have the gift of prophecy and can fathom all mysteries

and all knowledge, and if I have a faith that can move

mountains, but have not love, I am nothing. If I give all

I possess to the poor and surrender my body to the flames,

but have not love, I gain nothing. Love is patient, love is

Original edition published in English under the title *Love Never Fails*
by Lion Publishing, plc, Oxford, England. Copyright © Lion Publishing 2001.

North American edition published by Good Books, 2002. All rights reserved.

Picture acknowledgments

Cover, 14, 24: Images Colour Library. 6, 20, 28: SuperStock Ltd.
10: © David Barnes/Corbis. 12, 16: Powerstock Zefa. 26: The Image Bank.

Text acknowledgments

I Corinthians 13:1–8, from the *Holy Bible, New International Version*,
copyright © 1973, 1978, 1984 by International Bible Society.
Used by permission.

LOVE NEVER FAILS

Copyright © 2002 by Good Books, Intercourse, PA 17534
International Standard Book Number: 1-56148-367-2
Library of Congress Catalog Card Number: 2002024492

All rights reserved.
No part of this book may be reproduced in any manner,
except for brief quotations in critical articles or reviews,
without permission.

Printed and bound in Singapore.

Library of Congress Cataloging-in-Publication Data
Love never fails. -- North American ed.
    p. cm.
    ISBN 1-56148-367-2
    1. Bible. N.T. Corinthians, 1st, XIII, 1-8--Devotional literature.
I. Good Books (Intercourse, Pa.)
BS2675.54-L68 2002
242'.5--dc21   2002024492

love

never

fails

Good  Books™

Intercourse, PA 17534
800/762-7171 • www.goodbks.com

If I speak in the tongues of men and of angels, but have not love, I am only a resounding gong or a clanging cymbal.

I believe in love and compassion.

Mother Teresa of Calcutta

Some things you know with your mind, others with your soul.

Author unknown

Who you are speaks so loudly that I can't hear what you're saying.

Ralph Waldo Emerson

I want to know God's thoughts...

all the rest are details.

Albert Einstein

If I have the gift of
prophecy and can
fathom all mysteries
and all knowledge,

and
if I have
a faith
that can move
mountains,
but have not love, I am

One of the attributes of love,
like art, is to bring harmony
and order out of chaos, to
introduce meaning and effect
where before there was none,
to give rhythmic variations,
highs and lows to a landscape
that was previously flat.

Molly Haskell

nothing.

If I give all I possess
to the poor and
surrender my body

but have not love,
I gain nothing.

Among the attributes of God, although they are equal, mercy shines with even more brilliance than justice. Miguel de Cervantes

to the flames,

Our society makes us out of touch with ourselves. Annie Lennox

Love is
patient,
love is
kind.

I expect to pass through this life but once.

Therefore, if there be any kindness I can show,

or any good thing I can do for another

human being, let me do it now,

for I shall not pass this way again.

William Penn

It does not envy,
it does not boast,
it is not proud.

Man will do many things to get himself loved,

he will do all things to get himself envied.

Mark Twain

We do not judge the people we love.

Jean-Paul Sartre

We are shaped and fashioned
by what we love.

Johann Wolfgang von Goethe

God loves the world through us.

Mother Teresa of Calcutta

What can we gain by sailing to the moon
if we are not able to cross the abyss that
separates us from ourselves?

Thomas Merton

It is not rude,

it is not self-seeking,

it is not easily angered,

My own commitment is to a curious idea
put about by a carpenter turned dissident
in Palestine that the test of our humanity
is to be found in how we treat our enemies.

Paul Oestreicher

*it keeps
no record of
wrongs.*

Love does not

delight in evil

but rejoices

with the truth.

As scarce as truth is, the supply
has always been in excess of the demand.

Josh Billings

Virtue is not the absence of vices
or the avoidance of moral dangers;
virtue is a vivid and separate thing.

G.K. Chesterton

Goodness is the only investment that never fails.

Henry David Thoreau

Indifference is the strongest force in the universe.

It makes everything it touches meaningless.

Love and hate don't stand a chance against it.

Joan Vinge

It always protects, always trusts,

Peace, peace!

I am so mistrustful

of it: so much afraid

that it means a sort

of weakness and

giving in.

D.H. Lawrence

always hopes, always perseveres. I have learned to
use the word "impossible"
with the greatest caution.

Wernher von Braun

Hope is a state of mind.

It is not the same as joy that things are going well,
or willingness to invest in enterprises that are
obviously heading for success, but rather an ability
to work for something because it is good.

Václav Havel

Love
never

 *fails.*

The world is indeed
full of peril, and in
it there are many
dark places; but still
there is much that
is fair, and though
in all lands love is
mingled with grief,
love grows perhaps
the greater.

J.R.R. Tolkien

If I speak in the tongues of men and of angels, but have no love, I am only a resounding gong or a clanging cymbal. If I have the gift of prophecy and can fathom all mysteries and all knowledge, and if I have a faith that can move mountains, but have not love, I am nothing. If I give all I possess to the poor and surrender my body to the flames, but have not love, I gain nothing. Love is patient, love is